THE CHILDREN

THE CHILDREN OF YESTER
VICTORIA FLETCHER

ISBN 978-0-9576818-6-6

Designed and Published by MDPD
(enquiries@mdpd.co.uk)

*COVER IMAGES: Top – The Gate of Yester 2016.
Bottom – Yester Chapel "St Cuthbert's" (photograph courtesy of MDPD).*

THE CHILDREN OF YESTER

The right of Victoria Fletcher to be identified as the author of this work has asserted by her in accordance with the Copyright, Design and Patents Act 1988.

All rights are reserved. No part of this publication may be reproduced, stored in a retrieval system, or transmitted in any form by any means, electronic, mechanical, photocopying, recording or otherwise, without prior permission in writing from the author.

©Victoria Fletcher 2000
Revised Edition 2016

THE CHILDREN OF YESTER

ACKNOWLEDGEMENTS

My thanks go to Simon Kesley for encouraging me to re-publish this book and for promoting my recently published book 'The Other Side of Life' which has stimulated interest in this, my first, book.

To George Angus for photographing my old photos that appeared in the original publication and this revised edition.

To Jackie Borland for helping me with the corrections and proof reading.

To Roddy Martine for his eloquent synopsis of this book and its sequel.

Finally, to MDPD for designing and publishing this revised edition.

THE CHILDREN OF YESTER

CONTENTS

		Page
ACKNOWLEDGEMENTS		**3**
CONTENTS		**5**
LIST OF ILLUSTRATIONS		**6**
INTRODUCTION		**7**
CHAPTER I	**PART 1 - THE FAMILY**	**11**
	PART 2 - NURSERY ROUTINE	**23**
CHAPTER II	**PART 1 - CHRISTMAS AT YESTER**	**33**
	PART 2 - CHRISTMAS AFTER GRANDPA'S DEATH	**39**
	PART 3 - BOXING DAY	**41**
	PART 4 - CHRISTMAS WEEK	**43**
	PART 5 - NEW YEAR	**45**
CHAPTER III	**YESTER AT WAR**	**47**
CHAPTER IV	**ETIQUETTE AND MANNERS OF DAYS GONE BY**	**49**
CHAPTER V	**EVENTS, TRIALS & TRIBULATIONS**	**53**
CHAPTER VI	**SUMMER HOLIDAYS**	**55**
CHAPTER VII	**GRANDPA'S DEATH**	**59**
CHAPTER VII	**OPEN TO THE PUBLIC**	**61**

ILLUSTRATIONS

1. Yester Church
2. Yester House
3. Grandpa, 11th Marquis of Tweeddale and Hugo
4. Sally Churchill with Vicky Fletcher, Hugo, MaryAnne with Caroline and Jane Berry
5. Yester Chapel "St Cuthbert's"
6. Mummy, Hugo and Vicky
7. Children with toboggan – Sally Churchill, Jane Berry, Desmons Alexander
8. Nanny, Vicky and pram of dolls
9. Frances Coleridge
10. Yester house by Johnny Churchill
11. Hugo and Vicky on tricycle
12. Hugo and Vicky at North Berwick
13. Mummy (Lady Daphne Stewart) and I (Vicky) at Stewart Society dinner

THE GIFFORD WATER

"My heart beats faster
When I hear the Gifford Water
My head is filled with laughter
And I know that I am home"

INTRODUCTION

It's the morning before Christmas Eve 1948, and I and my elder brother Hugo are woken from our restless sleep beneath the prickly blankets on the top bunks of the sleeper train, by the sleeper attendant bringing tea and biscuits for my mother and us - a treat otherwise reserved for adults only. We unhitch the blind which shoots up the window with a snap to reveal that the train is coming into Waverley Station puffing clouds of smoke, and pulling up with a screech of brakes on wheels as it bumps against the buffers.

It's 6.30 a.m. and we have been travelling up all night since we left Somerset the day before, to return to our home at our Grandparents house in Scotland for Christmas. We excitedly eat the biscuits and peer out of the smoggy window at the awakening station, suitcases and parcels being piled onto porters trolleys and newspapers being sorted into sacks for delivery.

Having dressed hurriedly after a cold wash we step down gingerly off the high train steps into the foggy air of the platform where our large trunks are being unloaded from the guard's van, plus our collie dog 'Pinkie' and handed into capable hands of the chauffeur Rose waiting smilingly to meet us.

Once out in the snow covered streets of Edinburgh we really feel we have returned to Scotland where we were both born, but have left to go to schools 'down South' a custom started by King James I and VI, and to live

THE CHILDREN OF YESTER

with our mother on a farm in Somerset. Trams rush by on their silvery rails and horses pulling milk carts clatter over the cobbled street. Hugo and I sit with our faces glued to the window and count the Christmas trees lit up in the windows on opposite sides of the street - a competition carried on each year until well into our teens. The huge Christmas Tree lit up behind Princes Street neath the back drop of the Castle and Princes Street decorations. Christmas is here! Out of Edinburgh passing Musselburgh race course and the sea with its fresh salty air where lasses once gathered the mussels and cockles now sadly poisoned and dangerous to eat. As one drives up the A1 one can see far away on the left across the Forth, the hills of Fife and in front stretches the beautiful farming lands of East Lothian with Traprain Law, North Berwick Law, and the Bass Rock guarding Tantallon, the Douglas's stronghold, on the coast.

Through Tranent and on to Haddington, passing the bust of our Great Great Great Grandfather, the 8th Marquis of Tweeddale who introduced deep ploughing in East Lothian. Through the square and past the pink turreted 'genteel' George Hotel; Saint March the 'Lamp of Lothians', and

Yester Church

THE CHILDREN OF YESTER

over the Waterloo Bridge across the river Tyne out into the country and down towards Gifford. The snow covered Lammermuirs stretching behind the village nestling in the woods planted by my ancestors.

Once in Gifford we are greeted by the sight of the 18th century church built in 1708 especially for services of the reformed church and turn right down the Main Street past our friend Mr. Todds post office and Mrs. Hoggs Sweet Shop where Nanny went for our ration of sweets 'plus one or two more' during the war. Past the pub the 'Goblin Ha' and then opposite the Village Hall, originally the Parish School restored and reconstructed by the 10th Marquis of Tweeddale in 1887 on the occasion of Queens Victoria's Golden Jubilee. We turn left by the Tweeddale Arms and Ned Mullen's the butlers cottage, into the drive of Yester House, the Arms of the Tweeddales above the vacant wrought iron archway of the gates, alas melted down for gun fodder in the Second World War. On either side the little pink lodges to the house in which on one side lived Mr. Ainslie, the Forester and on the otherside Mr. Swanson also a Forester, next to the Gifford water which flows past Yester House.

Yester House

THE CHILDREN OF YESTER

As we go up the drive, with its magnificent beeches, some of the biggest in Scotland and where a huge oak once stood now panelling a room in Holyrood, with the sound of Gifford water on our right we come in sight of Yester House as we cross the bridge where the drive splits into the front and back drive, with its snow covered larches planted in 1739, at the end of the drive. My soul lifts and I know that I am home.

> " The Children of Yester were many
> Both animals and Children of man;
> They all lived happily together
> Played with each other and ran."

CHAPTER I - PART 1
THE FAMILY

My brother, Hugo David Montagu Fletcher, who was born in 1940, was the first boy to be born in the house since our Great uncle Lord Edward Hay who was born in 1888. He was grandpa's younger brother but sadly was killed in the Guard's Chapel in London when it was bombed during the Second World war whilst he was reading the lesson. He left two children Marioth and David Hay who were partly brought up by my grandmother, as their mother died when Marioth was only 8. Amongst her own and the vast number of other children Granny looked after before and during the war when there were sixteen of us in the house, each family with it's own nanny. Edward's grandson Charles is now the present Marquis as Grandpa's second brother Arthur was killed in the First World War and my mother told me that at the moment he was shot a scream as from a wounded horse was heard by all the Aunts, Granny and all the other ladies at that moment sitting knitting in the back drawing room, thereafter always hated by his namesake, Uncle Arthur Coleridge, Aunt Georgina's husband. Ned Mullen, in my time, the butler had gone away with him as batman in the First World War.

Sadly, Granny 'Midge' Tweedale who was brought up by our Great Grandpa Lewis Einstein - diplomat and writer - never had a son who lived,

THE CHILDREN OF YESTER

Grandpa, 11th Marquis of Tweeddale and Hugo

THE CHILDREN OF YESTER

since she miscarried her only boy 'Hugo' when rushing by train to the aid of a relative who was ill. Granny was small, dark, beautiful and vivacious and loved and was loved by the countless animals and children whom she looked after and was adored by all. Amongst her many adult admirers were both Noel Coward and Sean Leslie. My mother told me a story that when she was little and playing in the bushes of the drive at Hatchlands with Peter Cameron, one of Granny's 'adopted children', Sean Leslie arrived in a taxi which, however, he stopped and dismounted from at the bridge dividing the back and front drive, took off his shoes and socks and walked to the front of the house where the ladies were sitting on the lawn. He threw himself upon his knees in front of Granny and said 'Darling, I have walked barefoot from the station to greet you'. Another relative, Sir George Kennard told me he adored my grandmother so much that he used to follow her from room to room smoking the stubs of her cigarettes - cigarettes which alas eventually killed her since she smoked 60 a day and died of lung cancer at the age of 47 when I was only two years old.

Even at that early age, I have a loving memory of her since she frequently came to watch our 'bathtime' in the nursery wing and apparently on being told that she 'had died and gone away to heaven', I marched out onto the lawn and shouted 'God, you send my Granny back and mind she brings her cases too.'

I was not born at Yester but in the Nuffield hospital in Edinburgh because my mother was seriously ill with Goitre, and I was a fragile and tantrumous baby. My father got leave to fly from Drem where he was stationed at that time, to see me, and Nanny was appointed to look after Hugo and I since Mummy was obviously not well enough to do so. When she came for interview and to consider the post Hugo, who was a plump happy baby with long girlish looking hair, which Granny did not allow to be cut until he was two, was sitting in his pram and on seeing her stretched out his arms and said 'Nanny' quite winning her heart so she took the post, thus joining the other four nannies and 16 children and their mothers, all sheltering from the Second World war, in the house.

Hugo on the other hand was born in Yester House itself and Daddy ran all the way to the old castle 'The Goblin Ha' a mile away and built by our Gifford ancestor, Hugo de Gifford 'The Wizard' in the 15th century, in order to get water from its well to christen him with.

I too was christened at Yester on the 29th March, 1942 which was incidentally both my mother and father's birthday. It was performed by the

THE CHILDREN OF YESTER

Rev. Robert Dollar, Minister of Dunfermline Abbey and Bob Dollar was also a long standing friend and visitor to Yester House. I still have a lovely little New Testament given to me by him as is the custom. Hugo's son Gifford Morley Fletcher was the last of our family to be christened in Yester House in 1969.

Granny had four daughters:- Helen, Georgina, Daphne called 'Peanut', our mother, and Frances, the youngest who was sent to Canada for the duration of the war much to her chagrin especially since she returned to find her mother dying. Aunt Helen married Lionel Berry now Viscount Kemsley and had four daughters, after a splendid pre-war wedding with 22 bridesmaids, Mary Ann, Jane, Caroline and Katherine all looked after by Nanny 'Storey'.

Aunt Georgina married Arthur Coleridge who was a Barrister and then in the Irish Guards. They were the last people to be married in Yester Chapel "St Cuthberts". She, much the naughtiest and most amusing, had been the only daughter sent to school as she proved too much for the succession of French and German governesses to cope with, and as a result became a very successful journalist and Editor of 'Homes and Gardens' among other magazines and later she also wrote books on horse racing. Their home in London was bombed in the war so she was also living at Yester plus their only daughter Frances who became like a sister to me, and their Nanny, Nanna Collins arch enemy of the other country nannies.

Desmond Alexander and his brother, nephew of General Alexander, were also war refugees plus his mother 'Hero Alexander wife of Col. 'Baby' Alexander who commanded the O.C.T.V. at Dunbar. Also Sally Churchill aged 7, who was Winston Churchills' great niece and also my godparents son Oliver Walston.

When Granny became ill with cancer, Marjorie Nettlefold came to look after her brining with her, her brother Kenneth's four sons:- Timothy, Jeremy, Anthony and David plus their cousin David Starling son of Kenneth's sister Vivian. She also had an elder brother Teddy Wagg. Timothy and Jeremy and David Starling being teenagers lived in the main part of the house with the adults but Anthony and David, being our age, shared the nursery with us and their Nanny 'Nanny Wagg'.

Aunt Marjorie stayed after Granny's death and married Grandpa becoming Marchioness of Tweeddale and our step grandmother but still called 'Aunt Marjorie'. As well as the Aunts already mentioned, there was also staying in the house Granny Wagg - Aunt Marjorie's aged mother and

THE CHILDREN OF YESTER

Sally Churchill with Vicky Fletcher, Hugo, Mary Anne with Caroline and Jane Berry

Yester Chapel "St Cuthbert's"

THE CHILDREN OF YESTER

also our fierce Great Aunt Clementine Waring - Grandpa's sister. Another visitor always welcome in the nursery was Aunt Majorie's son by her previous marriage, Michael Nettlefold. He had lost one eye and both hands disposing of an exploded bomb and so had a fake fixed hand and a hook on the other and was known to us children as 'Captain Hook' which he accepted with good humour. He had a young wife Angie and sisters Rosemary and Penelope 'Penel', and later three children Charles, Julian and Tessa.

The rest of us children all lived in the nursery wing which was separated from the main house by a corridor and heavy swing door, and was run as a completely separate unit under the rule of the nannies and nursery maids. All the little children slept, ate and played there until they were old enough to graduate to having tea, then lunch and eventually dinner on special occasions with the adults in the main part of the house. I remember David Starling, Timothy and Jeremy were considered very grown up by me as they ate and spent most of their time in the main house though the two older Waggs were frequent visitors to the nursery.

The nursery wing consisted of two floors; at the top of which up some winding turreted stairs was a lovely round playroom in which there was a huge dolls house, with real lights that turned on and off and a lavatory with a chain that pulled, and a beautiful castle, a replica of Edinburgh castle, made by our grandfather as were my doll's cot and bamboo chairs and a miniature copy of Danskin Lodge which stood at the Duns Road old entrance to the Castle. There were also masses of fine lead soldiers both cavalry and infantry and guns which fired bullets like bits of lead pencil, with which the boys played war games endlessly whilst I carried the wounded away to the doll's house hospital. Other toys included a sweet shop complete with miniature filled jars and scales and a magnificent rocking horse, with a real mane and tail, saddle and bridle, on which two could ride, one of top of him, the other beneath, sitting on the platform between his legs and the rockers. The older boys used to ride it hard and fast until they tipped it up on its front rocker spilling off the little girls on the platform below. Around the walls were bookcases and glass fronted cases with stuffed birds and pinioned butterflies and a model of a 2lb salmon caught by my mother.

Down the winding wooden stair was the first floor main nursery with a large living room where we all ate and a freezing boys sleeping room and a smaller girls one plus the nursery bathroom/wash room and Nanny Baillie's bedroom. There were, however, blazing log fires with huge log boxes in the corridors and brass fenders and of course fire guards, and we all had much needed stone 'pig' hot water bottles to keep us from freezing in our brass ended beds. There was also a china potty beneath each bed for use at night and after breakfast and we were given pyjama cases to keep our night clothes in and to help us to learn to be tidy. The house was also heated by a huge main boiler down in the basement between the kitchen and the back door which fed the radiators situated beneath most of the windows and which was stoked by vast amounts of wood off the estate by Wattie the stoker.

All our clothes including the babies nappies which were not disposable in those days, were washed in the day nursery bathroom by the nursery maids by hand using a glass centred scrubbing board and wrung out in a mangle and then hung out to dry either on wooden clothes horses or out on a clothes line on the nursery lawn depending on the weather. Nanny liked all the table linen to be starched and I think did this herself and the young men's collars and cuffs. She was an expert at it and continued to starch linen for her neighbours in Haldane Avenue until she was over 85 years of age and completely bedridden. The ironing was done with flat irons heated beside the fire until electric irons came in when I was also given a miniature ironing board and small electric iron by Aunt Helen and Nanny taught both Hugo and me how to iron the most easy things like hankies and napkins at which Hugo excelled.

As we grew from babyhood into childhood we grew out of lovely white smocked dresses into skirts for girls and trousers mainly for the boys and dress kilts which they wore for smart occasions with white shirts and of course ties. We girls wore white liberty bodices and shirts underneath a black and white check tunic of 'shepherd's plaid' as tidy day clothes and of course dresses for parties with sashes and ribbons in our hair, mine which was pleated like several of the others. For scruffy play, we had khaki shirts and shorts and Uncle Kenneth still has a photo of his two younger boys and Hugo dressed like this with me standing at the end of the row looking as much like a boy as I could manage. We also later had thicker kilts for outdoor activities like shooting or walking in the woods or hills.

Clothes were passed down from one to another and lastly even to the larger dolls which nanny made clothes for. For a long time, Hugo wore a fawn pair of Sally Churchill's old corduroy trousers and would not give them up even after he went to Prep school until Nanny one day washed them with my red school knickers and they came out pink and that was the end of the trousers.

Grandpa sometimes joined us for tea which was then a special occasion since we would be sent up Grandpa's favourite ice cream from the main kitchen, and also would be allowed to set up the Hornby trains on the table plus rails and use their carriages to pass the butter and sugar round, and hope for derailments.

One of the things I remember in the Day Nursery and still have was an old carved drunk man leaning against a red windowed lamp post which lit up whilst he nodded his head from side to side and whistled 'Show me the way to go home' when wound up. Sadly now his bellows which propel the whistle are irrevocably broken. We all loved him and we was an old inmate of the nursery living room.

Halfway down a large flight of stone steps of the mathematical wrought iron bannistered staircase at the house end of the nursery corridor was a white barred window gate through which one climbed out onto the nursery lawn at the front of the house which was guarded by Mummy's flock of hissing geese plus her bantams and muskovy ducks which nested in the hole of a huge tree beside the pack leading from the chapel to the castle woods and Mummy's flock of goats on whose milk I was brought up since they discovered I was allergic to cows milk.

If one continued down the stairs past the loudly ticking grandfather clock one arrived at the basement floor and after passing the dairy went out through the nursery wing back door beside which was the locked gun room. In those days the dairy was a flourishing businesswith Jersey unpasteurised milk coming down in huge cans from the home farm at Yester Mains to be skimmed off its lovely thick cream which was sent up to the dining room and little round pats of individual butter portions were rolled between wooden pat boards. Cheese was also made in the still room next to the old Laigh Hall further down the main passage beneath the main house. Not only from cows milk but also from the goats which belonged to my mother, some of which were tethered on the lawn and were very naughty and had been known to butt the nannies when sitting on our swings. Around the dairy were beautiful blue and white Delft china cows which remained there long after the dairy ceased functioning. My mother once saw a ghost passing along the passage to the dairy. She followed the apparition thinking it was Aunt Marjorie until it disappeared up one of the blocked up stone turreted staircases.

Apart from the main staircases, there were four sets of turreted staircases

THE CHILDREN OF YESTER

at the corners of the main house, by which one could enter or leave any floor and climb to the attic much to the annoyance of the adults as we older children frequently used them to flit quickly out of sight no matter how often they were banned. These stairs were also surrounded by numerous little unused and ghostly dusty rooms ever waiting to be explored. My brother once declared he too saw a ghost in the rooms in the attic.

The main house was entered from the opposite end of the house to the nursery where originally the west wing had stood until burnt by fire in the 7th Marquises time and then finally demolished by the eighth Marquise. One now came in via the conservatory which set off a scent which pervaded the house. From there one entered the marble floored entrance hall pillared with pillars originally from the dining room from which the flower room, dogs room, library and Grandpa's business room all led off, then on down the passage separating the huge Robert Adam dining room, originally the front entrance of the house, from the double drawing room which looked out onto the grass tennis courts and park beyond. Next door to it was the yellow drawing room, a lovely bookcased and panelled room where certainly in winter time the adults spent most of the time, the double drawing room only being used on special occasions for entertaining on a

Mummy, Hugo and Vicky

large scale. Besides the yellow drawing room where two bedrooms, the larger with cherubs painted on the ceiling and this 'boudoir' my cousin Frances and I shared in later years.

Up the main staircase at the East end of the house were the suites of bedrooms and bathrooms surrounding the saloon or ball room which lay directly above the dining room and was so unsafe that the chandeliers beneath shook whenever someone walked across it. Beyond the saloon was a second set of stairs leading further up to the old governess' school room, the house keeper's room and the staff rooms. As its foot were suites of bedrooms used by the Wagg family and past them the Red room where my mother slept, all furnished with four poster beds and vast cupboards.

The saloon was the one room in the house many of the children were frightened off, particularly in the dark when we used to rush across it to gain the safety of the upper stair hallway and my cousin Frances once refused to join in a game of hide and seek because it entailed crossing the saloon in the dark. Years later when living in my flat in Edinburgh, but Tourist guiding at Yester at weekends, I had a dream about the house in which a mother hearing a scream rushed up the main staircase and across the saloon to see her son lying immobile at the foot of the upper stair balcony from which he had fallen to the floor beneath. If this ever actually happened to one of our predecessors I do not know, but if it had it might well be the reason for our abhorrence of the spot.

The basement of the main house was reached by the pantry stairs, which lay between the dining room and the pantry, or by one of the corner turreted stairs and also via the nursery mathematical stairs mentioned previously. The pantry and dining room were presided over by Ned Mullen, the butler (who had gone to the First World War with our Great Uncle Arthur Hay) now an aged and much loved and respected member of the household, as was his wife Mrs Mullen. In the pantry was a huge walk in silver safe into which all the silver was put every night and after each meal, and a fascinating knife sharpening machine which one turned with a handle to sharpen the knives stuck in to it. There was a service lift down from the pantry to the kitchen beneath, by which the food was sent up from the kitchen below.

The kitchen was run by Mrs Sinclair a large, comfortable and kindly cook who sat in a huge arm chair in a corner of the vast room, between meals and listened to Scottish music on the wireless surrounded by two large well fed tabby cats and copper weights and measures and sets of scales. We used to love to visit her, the boys to play with the weights and measures and me to dance to the reels and strathspeys she used to listen to on her wireless, and both to scrounge for extra mince pies between meals on the 'Twelve Days of Christmas', all forbidden by our step grandmother who believed children should be out of doors and not in the kitchen beneath the servants feet.

In later years by the time the home was open to the public the main kitchen was closed and a small one built into Aunt Frances' old bedroom which lay off the corridor between the main house and the nursery.

As for the rest of the house; the cleaning was done by a vast army of dailies who lived in the village and walked, or bicycled up the drive each day like Ned, to clean the house first thing every morning and to take early morning tea to the adults and to open their curtains, stoke the boiler and lay and light the huge fires, and fill the log boxes with wood sawn on the estate and the men also the bring in the garden produce and game from the woods. At night all the wooden shutters on the windows had to be closed, curtains drawn and beds turned down ready to get into. But all these servants were treasured and respected friends who had worked and lived on the estate for generations and considered it as much theirs as ours.

THE CHILDREN OF YESTER

MY NANNY

"I love to see my Nanny
She loved me as a child
Her ever lasting kindness
Her never fading smile"

CHAPTER I - PART 2
NURSERY ROUTINE

    Days in the nursery followed a quiet routine, depending on the weather. After "sweets" followed by a rest on our beds after lunch, we often went for a walk in the afternoon with Nanny. We loved to go up to the home farm, 'Yester Mains', to watch the cows being milked and to see the lovely Jersey calves, one of whom 'Rosemary' danced in her pen when we sang to her. On the right where the stalls for the dairy cows and the square pens for the calves, and behind a huge sliding door the box where the big Jersey bull lived. He was said to be dangerous and had once chased the cattleman out of his field making him jump the hedge in fear of his life. Originally the cows were milked by hand and one always wanted to have a try at squirting the milk into the bucket whilst squatting on the three corned legged stools and squeezing the cows soft teat. In later years they were milked electronically by huge suckers which were clamped onto their teats.
    On the left side of the farm road were the large stone sheds for the bullocks, along the front passage of which one could walk through and watch them munching the turnips they were fed on in the long mangers which ran the length of the passage. There were also still two large cart horses with feathery legs kept for ploughing and an old pony and a saddle room with all the harness, blinkers, brasses and decorations they wore for showing.

THE CHILDREN OF YESTER

Near the farm which also had sheep in the surrounding fields was the saw mills where one could watch the huge timbers from the woods being sliced like cakes by the semi circular saws midst the heavy scent of sawdust so different from that or the steaming cattle and smell of turnips of the farm.

There were also friends in the cottages on the farm to drop in and visit as all over the estate.

However our favourite place to walk up to have tea was at the Gifford end of the front drive where one turned right up the hill past one of the lodges to walk to Sunnyside the home of the gamekeeper 'John Brown' and his daughter Mrs Campbell. On route all the children used to pick the hips and haughs for them to make jelly out of and when we arrived there was always a warm welcome and pancakes and scones with strawberry jam for tea.

John Brown organised all the shoots, for which young and old on the estate used to beat, and also any fishing on the river where there was

Children with toboggan - Sally Churchill, Desmond Alexander and Jane Berry

abundant trout. Most of the shoots took place on the Lammermuirs where there were grouse, though much depleted by disease during the war, and also pheasants in the woods who were fed plus the vermin kept down by among other ways ferrets kept in wooden cages near the house.

Many wild berries grew in the woods and we used to go on wild strawberry picking expeditions though I doubt less than half got back to the nursery to be made into jam. Also oddly enough red currents and gooseberries grew in the woods above the back drive and were a welcome snack between meals for us as foraging older children in later years.

Here on the banks above the back drive we used in winter to run the sledge - a proper ice toboggan - with front boggies - down the hill towards the chicken runs beneath, sometimes crashing into their wire fences when not able to stop in time, sending up a flurry of chickens. But this was when we were older and no long Nanny controlled. In our mothers childhood a pony was used to make an ice trail down the bank for them to slide down by towing a water bucket over the snow, but we had to be content with the snow itself or that failing the bare slippery grass.

We had a pony "Black Beauty" a tiny Shetland stallion who was delivered into the dining room in a packing case one Christmas morning as a present for my brother. He was very intelligent and learnt to be ridden by us two children on a sheepskin saddle made by Mummy and driven in harness by my Mother travelling along on skis behind him in the bad winter of 1947 and also to pull a small dog cart which we all sat in better weather. He was taught to do tricks; to stand up on his hind legs and to lie down and die for the King - all performed at a fete at the end of the war in aid of the Red Cross, and League of Pity for Children of which our Great Aunt Clemy was president since a child. My brother had a little Rifle Brigade uniform, our father's regiment, made for the occasion and I wore a nurses uniform complete with red crossed apron.

Alas Black Beauty came to a sad end. He lived in a field with a large horse Benny, who belonged to my Mother, and was fed a pail full of corn each day, under whose tummy, the tiny stallion would stand at feeding time and snatch the odd mouthful whilst the larger horse drew breath. One day Benny was off his feed, the greedy little pony scoffed the lot and that night died of colic despite Mummys and the vets attempts to save him.

Benny was a remarkably placid seventeen hand high horse. At Haddington Horse Show having ploughed his way through the novice jumps with Mummy he then proceeded to win the 'open' jumping competition.

THE CHILDREN OF YESTER

Sally Churchill, then aged seven, asked Mummy if she could jump Benny in the Handy Hunter competition. Mummy said yes if she could control him over the few small practice jumps at the side of the ring. These they jumped successfully and entered the competition during which horse and child were seen to be speeding up to a huge five bar gate they were meant to open as part of the competition. However they jumped it clear to the delight of the crowds though not to the delight of the judges, nor Mummy who feared he was running away with her. Afterwards having completed the rest of the obstacles successfully and asked what happened at the gate, Sally explained she realised she was too small to bend down and open it from Bennys full height and was unable to mount such a big horse on her own if she dismounted to open it, so decided the only alternative was to jump it, which she did. Benny was very friendly and would canter up if whistled to in the field and stop dead at ones feet disconcerting Nanny who was afraid of and did not really like horses and called him a 'clumsy beast'. It was at Haddington Show that Hugo got kicked on the knee by a strange horse and had to have it bandaged up with elastoplast. Nanny then went away for two weeks holiday - the only one I can remember - leaving us with a temporary Nanny who was given instructions to remove the bandage in ten days time. However the dear little boy would not let her touch it and so it was still there when Nanny returned to remove it forthwith without any nonsense. This Nanny also fell into my bad books as she attempted to wash my face with soap, a thing never done before - or since. So we were all delighted when she left as I think she must have been too.

Later when I was 5 I too was given an Exmoor pony "Butterfly" for my last birthday at Yester and I can remember walking down the drive to fetch her from Gifford and her pulling poor Nanny over bruising her knees and tearing her smooth Lyle stockings further adding to her dislike of horses and ponies. Butterfly ate too much and was very prone to Lamenitis, though Butterfly lived long enough to go to boarding school with me in England when I was six.

After tea in the nursery we would be washed and changed into tidy pretty clothes and taken through to the main house to spend a short time with the adults before our baths and bed. One of the things I can remember is my aunt Frances grey poodle who used to lie in wait beneath the sofa and nip children's ankles which apparently offended him. Granny on the other hand had a huge placid dog which used to carry use tiny children around the room on his back and Grandpa had a cuddly white poodle with pink eyes.

THE CHILDREN OF YESTER

The adults in their turn would visit us at bath time especially Granny who picked me up and cuddled me whenever I cried to nannies slight chagrin who used to tell her I was spoilt, but it was eventually discovered that not only was I intolerant to cows milk and had to be fed on goats milk but also that I had Mesenteric Adenitis, and one of my earliest memories is of a doctor leaning over me and prodding my abdomen in his small dark surgery in Edinburgh. So I maintain I was crying because of abdominal pain.

Later tea was the first meal we attended in the main house. It was not eaten at the dining room table but at a smaller table at right angles to it and Aunt Marjorie sat resplendent in front of a huge silver tea pot over a burner which one blew out with silver trumpet to the children's great enjoyment. All the poodles, of which she had several black ones got a drink of tea, out of the lovely bone china deep saucers, put like everyone else but on the floor of course. Butter at tea was served on a large pot of water to keep it cool, with home made raspberry or strawberry jam and a lovely sticky chocolate cake to be eaten after pancakes, scones and small triangular sandwiches with the crusts cut off and Selkirk bannock, a round flat loaf with sultanas in it.

The only time when our visits to the main house were curtailed was when we all in the nursery got whooping cough and were segregated from the main house in case anyone, but especially Grandpa contracted it. It was during this holiday that Angela Nettlefold staying in the main house, one day saw a little girl in a Victorian dress standing in the passageway between the main house and nursery and thought she was seeing a ghost, as till then she had been unaware that there were any children in the house at all. That little ghost was me.

Grandpa loved children but used to tease us with the maxim "children should not only be seen and not heard but also not seen and not heard".

The only other time I can remember illness at Yester was when my brother Hugo contracted scarlet fever and was sent to the local Haddington Fever Hospital. As I was in contact I, though only eighteen months old, was sent along too. Imagine the fury of my ex nurse step grandmother when on visiting her grandchildren she found her dear little grand daughter crawling about uncontrolled in and out the diphtheria wards! Since I had been inoculated I did not actually contract diphtheria, but instead caught measles as a result of which my eye sight was severely affected and I had to wear glasses at a very early age since I crawled straight into unseen walls.

When we were ill with coughs and colds Nanny and Dr Bannerman our

THE CHILDREN OF YESTER

GP were great believers in the healing powers of Vic and Friars Balsam, the former which Nanny would rub on our chest taking it out of a little blue glass jar and the latter which was applied in a steaming aluminium bowl of hot water which we would sit and bend over, with our heads covered in towels, breathing in the strong aroma. Hugo also was fed lovely green Minadex for some reason and the rest of us malt extract which we all loved and were given each day after breakfast.

Evenings in the nursery were spent quietly either reading or being read to. Grandpa gave us the Ali Baba books and I was given Black Beauty illustrated by Lionel Edwards. We also were given by Nanny the Little Black Sambo books which were actually written by the mother of our general practitioner Dr Bannerman. There was a French illustrated book "Gideon" all about a family of foxes who were the villains of the farm in the story and were always coming to gruesome or amusing ends. Hugo read this as he could read French at a very early age. The other nursery books I remember were "Strewal Peter" with his long finger nails, and "Little Lord Fontelroy"

Nanny, Vicky and pram of dolls

THE CHILDREN OF YESTER

which I read and which is still a favourite of mine and Hugos "Gullivers Travels in Lilliput", where the people had a war between those who cracked the broad end of a boiled egg and those who attacked it from the sharp end. Needless to say we started at the broad end which Nanny neatly sliced off for the little children. The eggs were kept in a beautiful porcelain chicken plus tray on which stood eight chick egg cups which we ate our eggs out of - dyed red, brown or blue by nanny at Easter time. Mummy still has this at Blainslie and I was given a white one by an Arab princess friend of ours, Princess Musbah Haider, in memory of it but mine does not have the chick egg cups.

Between tea and supper we also often played snakes and ladders, ludo, tiddley winks, draughts, dominoes, halma or cards with Nanny, snap and happy families when we were small progressing to racing demon a great family favourite and later canasta, both of which we sometimes played with the adults in the main house. There were also wonderful jigsaw puzzles of many hundreds of pieces which Hugo excelled in and has enjoyed doing ever since. Grandpa also did these alone and with Hugo. He taught Hugo how to play chess and later piquet which he excelled at. Grandpa had also played piquet with his younger brother Eddy Hay before he was killed.

In the daytime I often played with my dolls of which I had several different types; firstly a wooden one with a red cape given me by Nanny and called 'Catherine', a plastic squashy one chosen by Hugo "because I had no boys", a valuable china headed doll which I detested and a large soft rag doll made for me by Nannies mother. Also Aunt Marjorie won for me in a raffle a lovely doll with eyes that opened and shut and who said "Mama" which Nanny made a beautiful dress for out of an old one of mine. Granny also gave me a toy furry monkey and I also had a golliwog. Finally when Daddy returned from the war he brought me a lovely doll complete with collapsible high chair. In the nursery there were beautiful sets of red and white Russian wooden dolls which fitted into one another.

Frances Colendge and I used to play doctors and nurses in the downstairs day nursery. Frances always being the unwitting patient who was fed countless innocuous 'medicines' concocted by me who at an early age had decided to be a doctor or at least a nurse. Hugo on the other hand wished to be a 'rolly' driver amongst other things like fireman and train driver.

I also had four sets of miniature china tea sets with which I had tea parties and served 'real tea' to all partakers i.e. tea without mile like the adults.

THE CHILDREN OF YESTER

Frances Coleridge

THE CHILDREN OF YESTER

One of these sets Daddy brought back from Italy, another 20 century set was given me for Christmas by aunt Marjorie made in Torquay and had epigrams and rhymes on the larger pieces like 'The cup that cheers' and 'Little boy blue come blow up your horn'. But I also had two much earlier sets and 18 century 'Green Maiden Hair Fern' Ridgway dinner service complete with Achettes and soup tureen and a blue Ridgways coffee/tea service with attractive picture in blue of houses and willow trees and people out of Charles Dickens' Old Curiosity Shop. All of which I still have. Mummy also gave me a lovely miniature breakfast set on a tiny tray.

On rainy days we could exercise on a set of rings and ropes hung in the nursery corridor or learn to make things with plasticine and later papier mache which Mummy taught us. We also played with Hugo's trains and meccano sets or peered through the kalaidescopes and lanterns and slides in the top nursery. Later when we were older we used to play ping pong endlessly and also a football toy game with opposing teams which kicked a ball when you pulled the rungs. Nanny herself played patience endlessly and Mummy taught us to build card houses which kept us occupied for hours and we also played Totopoly a racing game made by the makers of Monopoly which Aunt Marjories gave Hugo for Christmas and another game called Farming.

Nanny also sometimes made Tablet which Hugo and I also learnt to make and used to give as Christmas presents to the aunts and uncles much to the detriment of their teeth as ours tended to turn out more like toffee. Nanny also taught us to knit. She herself knitted many of the clothes. Hugo became quite good and learnt 'plain and pearl' I with my bad eye sight only achieved plain. The adults also knitted jerseys with lovely sheep and horse patterns, Aunt Helen using an expensive knitting machine even made kilts and Mummy who had a spinning wheel spun the sheeps wool. Nanny also used an old treadle sewing machine and I had a little weaving set with which I weaved my dolls blankets and scarves. Grandpa and Granny did beautiful tapestry seats for the chairs including one at Holyrood.

In the nursery there were special phrases typical of each of us. Nannies was 'For the love of Mike', usually used when exasperated to which Hugo usually replied "Who's Mike?" but we never did find out. We all used the excuse 'Nanny 'lows me' when we hoped to get away with some dubious deed in the presence of another adult and I think this originated from the day Nanny arrived and found Sally Churchill standing on the nursery mantelpiece to test the new Nannies mettle. Anthony Waggs favourite was

THE CHILDREN OF YESTER

'What all by myself' when he did not want to do something and doubtless there were many more which I have forgotten. Anthony liked teasing little girls especially me whom he used to recite the rather nasty poem out of Strewal Peter.

"Little Willies only six,
sat in the fire and
played with sticks"

"Little Willie in his bright blue sashes
Fell into the fire and
was burnt to ashes"

"Now though the room grows chilly
We haven't the heart
To poke poor Willie"

    Needless to say we were not allowed to play with fire which always had a guard in front of it.

    After meals we all said "Please may I be excused and get down" and one other thing I can remember is that if a stalk of tea floated to the top of ones cup we believed 'a stranger' guest was coming. The boys also used to tease us girls with nanny as an accomplice if we ate the last of anything - say the last pancake. Then one was told to keep silent whilst eat it and earn "A handsome husband and ten thousand a year" which silence the boys would try and make us break. All the other girls won their husbands except me so perhaps I could not keep silent.

CHAPTER II - PART 1
CHRISTMAS AT YESTER

Christmas at Yester started on Christmas Eve decorating the tree, in which as little nursery children we did not partake having been sent early to bed in expectancy of the coming of Santa Claus.

In those days the tree was decorated by the adults, and older children living in the main house i.e. the older Waggs and David Starling, but later we helped too.

It was a magnificent full size tree brought in off the estate and placed in the corner near the middle door of the back drawing room and hung with silver tinsel, 'snow', gold balls and candles which were lit for all to see on Christmas afternoon plus in later years fairy lights, Santa Clauses etc.

For us small children, Christmas really started on Christmas morning with waking in the night, hearing a scuffle, scrambling down to the foot of one's bed to anxiously feel one's stocking hung up the evening before. 'Had one been good enough, had Father Christmas really come?' A quick feel, 'yes it was filled to the brim and bulged with different shapes and sizes.' A contented sigh and snuggle back into ones pillows beneath blankets and a thick eiderdown to awake at dawn and wait for the permitted time of opening. Traditionally our stockings always had a Tangerine/Clementine at the heel and a bit of coal at the foot. Usually a bag of chocolate gold covered coins, a walnut and other small, some not so small presents usually including puzzle games and toys like 'yo yos' on strings, mouth organs, and stuff for blowing your own balloons etc. depending on your age.

One of the first Christmas mornings I can remember is one in which Cousin Francis Coleridge and I were the only children sleeping in the nursery, actually in the boys freezing dormitory in whose grate her parents had insisted a huge fire be lit before we went to bed, to warm up the room. Her father Uncle Arthur dressed up as Father Christmas and by that age we were old enough to peep and enjoy his get up including white flowing beard. He had been an amateur actor before the war and so was well up to the part.

Another year I remember was when I was much older and sleeping in the main house in a bedroom at the far end of the West corner of the house in the corridor in which Grandpas dressing room was. Mummy was in the identical room in the East corridor called the 'Red room where she slept in a four poster bed, both corridors ending at a door leading to one of the small turret staircases at the four corners of the house between the bedrooms and the en suite bathrooms with a huge bath and china wooden seated lavatory, which when one was small one was scared one would fall down, and old fashioned chain pull.

Hugo and I joined Mummy at 8 o'clock, when one of the house maids appeared to pull her curtains and shutters and bring her early morning tea tray. A tin of biscuits and a glass of water already having been provided for each adult when they arrived to stay, plus writing paper and envelopes. Together we would open our stockings all sitting on the bed and by this time we had often contributed to Mummy's stocking in the form of Knitting Nancy mats. The Knitting Nancys having been obtained in some previous years stocking.

That Christmas was always to be remembered by the fact that Mummy had also brought her small Boston Bull Terrier 'Quigley' to stay with us, but Aunt Marjorie took a dislike to her and would not let her come downstairs and join the assembled company and other dogs. Quigley took her revenge on being left alone in the room, by opening a box of 'After Eight' chocolates Mummy had been given in her stocking and strewing half sucked chocolates all over the room and the sofa cushions etc. and eating the rest. After Christmas morning breakfast we all went to church. The children with Nanny to our local church in Gifford. The adults with Grandpa and Aunt Marjorie to St Marys Presbyterian Church in Haddington - our

THE CHILDREN OF YESTER

local 'county town' of which Grandpa was an elder.

Gifford Church was a lovely little 18th century white church standing at the Haddington end of Gifford. The Tweeddale family sat in the gallery which is opposite the old pulpit which came from the original collegiate church of St Cuthberts which stands next to the present Yester House and in which pulpit John Knox once preached. The Minister appears at the beginning of the service from the hidden door in the wooden screen next to the pulpit, in an exciting manner for the children.

The village children who usually sat in the front rows of the main aisle nearest to the pulpit; at Christmas, sang at least the first verse of 'Away in a Manger' and they all brought toys and presents for children in need. The Minister at that time was Mr Cummings who was known for his long sermons interspersed with prolonged "Aaands".

When my Grandfather was a small boy; the shepherds used to bring their dogs to church with them - each lying beside his master. One Sunday my Grandfather took a live rabbit to church with him, concealed under his Eton jacket. In the middle of the sermon he dropped the unfortunate rabbit from the gallery into the body of the church. Imagine the fun and consternation as the rabbit ran round the church hotly persued by the excited sheep dogs, and the people since the Minister in fury roared, "remove the rabbit and remove Lord Gifford"! My Grandfather who was duly chastised said it was well worth it, but sadly that was the end of the sheep dogs going to church.

After walking back down the drive to the House we all got washed and tidied for Christmas lunch in the main house along with all the cousins, aunts, grannies and great grannies.

Lunch consisted of a huge turkey, bred by Aunt Marjorie, but whose hated duty it was off the elder children to shut up the birds each night often prolonged by the birds going up trees at dark instead of into their sheds, roast turkey plus all the usual trimmings including sausages, bacon, roast potatoes, brussel sprouts and lashings of bread sauce. One of the children was usually given the 'wish bone' or breast bone of the turkey - as with chicken - and had the added treat of pulling it with the person of their choice - in my case Grandpa - and making ones chosen 'wish'. The Christmas pudding was then brought in, flaming, on a silver salver, by Ned the butler and served with brandy butter and filled with silver three penny bits and traditional small but usually silver charms which one excitedly poked around for in ones pudding.

THE CHILDREN OF YESTER

Lunch ended with Christmas crackers, pulled with ones neighbour, also filled with charms and small presents including rings and even bracelets one of which I wore at parties for years afterwards. Also paper jokes and sayings which were read out to the assembled company the adults joining in the fun and all putting on their paper hats.

After lunch Nanny took all the children out for a walk and returned just before three o'clock to join the adults in the back drawing room. The tree was lit up, Ned standing by with a silver snuffer in case of fire, and everyone's presents were arranged in separate piles usually a chair each or two to three to a sofa. We then all listened to the Kings Christmas message at three o'clock which always ended with "God Save the King" during which everyone especially the young and fit were expected to stand to attention. This was followed by nine carols and lessons from Kings College Cambridge during which time we were allowed to open our long looked forward to presents - including one from the dogs who also got presents; boneos etc. all wrapped up in Christmas paper which Aunt Marjorie used to collect up, smooth out and fold to keep for future use. We then played happily with our presents till tea at 4 pm in the dining room with the grown ups when there was always a lovely Christmas cake with white icing and decorated with a miniature Santa Claus sledge and team of reindeer. We also could choose, Scotch bun, a black heavy fruit cake encased in pastry, typical to Scotland.

If I remember correctly we then, if old enough i.e. over five, had a rest before bathing and changing excitedly for dinner in evening dress in the dining room with the adults in the main house. Party or long dress for the girls and ladies, and kilts or black tie for the boys and men, failing that at least suits or school uniform but usually all were correctly dressed.

Dinner was a formal affair started by Grandpa walking from the yellow room, where the grown ups had drinks prior to dinner, with the first lady guest on his arm followed by the other adults two and two and lastly the children. The first lady always sat on Grandpas right and the principal male guest on Aunt Marjories right, at the far end of the table. When old enough to eat regularly in the dining room on less formal occasions I often sat next to Aunt Marjorie so that she could supervise my manners and ensure that I ate the hated grouse and cold meat which I also disliked and did not take too much of the lovely thick Jersey cream. She had a bell at her feet which she pressed when it was time for Ned to bring in the next course and as a treat I was sometimes allowed to press this. At breakfast, which apart from tea was the least formal of meals one was allowed to sit on Grandpas left and maybe on ones birthday even to sit in the place of honour on his right.

Dinner ended after Christmas mince pies or brandy snaps with 'dessert' on beautiful porcelain plates with nectarines, peaches, figs and grapes and crystallised fruit and ginger, all eaten with gilded desert knives and forks, not the fingers. Grapes also being cut off the bunch with ornate silver scissors. All the fruit off course coming from the ancient garden greenhouses of which there were two main ones both heated by huge water pipes. Each person was supplied with a glass fingerbowl to dip ones sticky fingers in and dry on ones huge slippery starched white damask napkins which seemed to have a greater propensity for the floor rather than the children's knees.

The men were served with port and the ladies with liqueurs and there was always a toast 'to the King', or 'Queen' after which Grandpa and the men smoked cigars and the ladies cigarettes and if we had not already had them at lunch we pulled crackers and ate nuts, marrons glace and chocolates whilst the grown ups drank black coffee with or without cream from beautiful dainty armorial cups after which the day ended for us children by a short prayer kneeling by ones bed before going to sleep.

One year when aunt Marjorie was ill in bed at Christmas and Aunt Alice, Uncle Teddy's wife, was first lady, with Hugo still a little boy sitting next to her, she gave him so much kummel that he ended up giggling and rolling under the table to Aunt Marjories fury when it eventually reached her ears the following day. I also was given kummel for the first time and can remember its strong aniseed taste to this day.

NED (THE BUTLER)

"Ned escaped being filled with lead;
Ned's hands shook, but not his head;
Ned rang the gong; 'time to be fed'
Ned shut the shutters and so to bed."

THE CHILDREN OF YESTER

CHAPTER II - PART 2
CHRISTMAS AFTER GRANDPA'S DEATH

When we were in our late teens and lived with our Stepfather, Col. F. Robin Stewart, 'Fa', on his small farm 'Middle Blainslie', near Lauder, we used to drive over to Yester on Christmas day in the landrover for either Christmas lunch or Christmas dinner. Often this meant driving through deep snow which my Stepfather was experienced in and usually good at. But one year we left earlier in the car with Mummy, since he was not ready, expecting him to follow on in the landrover, however he did not arrive until well after lunch time having skidded and half turned over into the ditch on our side road off the A68. This was in the years before the pass over Soutra was changed and it very often became blocked with snow and drivers were totally dependent on the huge snow plough that patrolled it regularly during the winter season, but even then sometimes in a blizzard, the snow would build up so much that even the big snowplough could not get through and Soutra would be closed for days.

The last Christmas I remember at Yester is one which I and Aunt Marjorie were the only people sleeping in the house. This was soon after my Grandfathers death in 1967.

At that time I was working as a physiotherapist in the City Hospital in Edinburgh and living in a flat in Regency Terrace. I had a very old red mini at the time, my first car. My friend Patty Martine asked me to go with her to the midnight carol service at St. Giles on Christmas eve, and since I was working that day and the weather had been mild with little or no snow I accepted.

So having finished work and tidied my flat; I packed my case plus the presents I was taking, and set off with my Boston Bull Terrier dog 'Bear' who accompanied me everywhere even to work. The midnight service in St. Giles was a wonderful start to Christmas, the huge cathedral was packed and the congregation joined in the carol singing lustily and there was a great feeling of Christmas all around.

After the service, we came out to find that it had started to snow but I set off for Gifford and Yester via Dalkeith and Penciatland driving as usual past the Christmas trees lit up in the peoples windows and arrived at Yester where there was a lovely thin carpeting of snow everywhere.

Since it was late at night, Aunt Marjorie had already locked up and shuttered the main house, but had left the side door that led past the old gun room into the nursery wing, open. Bear and I crept in the dark as quietly as we could and set off up the old stone mechanical staircase which led to the nursery and passage to the main house. Bear suddenly stopped dead in his tracks, hackles rising, and refused to go a step further. Nothing would move him, he seemed to be seeing an apparition in front us and though I could see nothing I had the feeling that there was something barring his way, so I picked him up and together we passed safely into the passage to the main house, past the present small modern kitchen which previously had been aunt Frances' bedroom, through the heavy green fire door into the main lit up house.

The next day, after a quiet breakfast alone with Aunt Marjorie the rest of the Blainslie party joined us for Christmas lunch; with Ned the faithful old butler still waiting on us though now with slow tread and shaking hand, and the day proceeded as in times gone by though on a smaller scale, the others leaving after Christmas tea after which Aunt Marjorie and I shut the heavy shutters on all the main downstairs windows, Ned having done the upstairs, we had a quiet dinner and so to bed.

CHAPTER II - PART 3
BOXING DAY

Boxing day at Yester was the day for the estate children's party; which was a huge party held in the back drawing room. The children came with their parents, all dressed up for the occasion in their party dresses, the little boys usually wearing kilts and white shirts or their school uniforms.

First their was tea; with pancakes, scones, sandwiches, brandy snaps and cakes, and jelly and ice cream and crackers and balloons for everyone who then put on their paper hats.

Next Father Christmas arrived and every single child got a present including us. Good useful presents. One year I got a water colour paint box which I still have and Hugo was given oil painting by numbers, another year a little weaving set with which I wove blankets for my miniature dolls cot and a scarf. The estate children were given similar things, pencil cases, a box of 50 colouring pencils, puzzles and games and dolls and teddies for the smaller children.

This was followed by party games, 'pass the parcel', 'I sent a letter to my love', 'blind mans buff', 'oranges and lemons', 'the farmers in his den', progressing to, 'the grand old duke of York'. I hated 'oranges and lemons' because of the bit 'and cut of your head', which frightened me but we all enjoyed the tug of war at the end of it and following in a chain after 'in and

THE CHILDREN OF YESTER

out the dusty windows'.

When we were a bit older - ten or so - we were often entertained in the huge saloon upstairs, all sitting on chairs we watched either a funny film, 'Laurel and Hardy' or Charlie Chaplin or when a bit younger I remember a very good magician coming and doing marvellous tricks including producing real live white furred rabbits out of his top hat. We also had the original Lassie film.

CHAPTER II - PART 4
CHRISTMAS WEEK

    Between Christmas and New year we would go to their children's parties in the neighbouring 'big houses' dotted around the county, including Gosford, home of the Earl of Wemyss whose daughter Elizabeth my brother Hugo was enamoured with. We went with Nanny driven by the chauffeur as did most of the other children and it was considered 'de trop' to arrive with ones parents.

    We were also taken to films and pantomines in Edinburgh including 'Peter Pan' after which we called Michael Nettlefold 'Captain Hook' but the player I liked best and remember in it was the huge Wendy dog. We also went to the film 'Red Shoes' with Moira Sheeragh at the end of which I cried copiously. Another pantomime I can remember was one in which the compere kept trying to get us children to join in and Hugo who was very bright answered most of his quipps and questions both he and I standing on our seats in the stalls as were both still very little.

    Conversely when Nanny took us to the film 'Laddie son of Lassie' we wept loudly and copiously in all the sad bits so that Nanny cried "If you're going to greet, I'll take you home" to which we replied "No, no we're loving it" and stayed till the end when all turned out happily ever after like most children's films. In those days films in public places were always preceded by 'God save the King' during which everyone respectfully stood to attention.

Children's parties progressed to children's dances as we grew older and which we had been prepared for by going to dancing classes at which Nanny told me Hugo always made a bee line for the prettiest girl, I suspect Elizabeth Charteris again. The first one I can remember was at the Georgian house 'Eaglescairnie' which at that time belonged to the Bell family who were mine owners. I was too young to dance so sat in a white party dress on the sofa with the other tiny girls, but I can still picture a boy in a green kilt dancing in the middle of an eightsome reel circle.

Years later I went to a dance in aid of 'Save the Children' which my step Grandmother was president off. I wore a silk pink crinoline which had been made for one of my forebears and since it was a bit long my partner persistently trod on it! I also had a yellow and black velvet Tudor dress which my Grandmother had made for her to wear at an Edinburgh pageant when she played the part of Mary Queen of Scots at Craigmillar. This I also wore as Mary Queen of Scots at a fancy dress horse show in the Borders for which I had to learn to ride side saddle.

The days between Christmas and New year were spent writing thank you letters and helping the adults gather up the autumn leaves into beehived shaped heaps and making bonfires which we lit the first day using paper and matches and thereafter attempted to keep it going for as many days as one could without using another match - a practice at which my Aunt Georgina excelled.

If there was snow we built snowmen with pebbles for eyes, carrots for their noses and complete with buttons (pebbles again) on their coats, hat and scarf and naturally played snowballs. We tobogganed down the back drive bank and in the bad winter of 1947/48 I can remember standing on the back of my aunt Frances' skis as she skied gently along the drive on the exceptionally deep snow that fell that year.

CHAPTER II - PART 5
NEW YEAR

New Year at Yester was celebrated by a formal dinner I the evening rather like that at Christmas but with a piper to pipe in the New Year and in my younger days sometimes with a dance for family and people of the estate.

The first dance I can remember, other than the one at Eaglecairnie already mentioned, was one of these. I can remember the thrill of coming down the main Yester staircase in a real evening dress, a pink taffeta one, and joining the large assembly of people in the dining room which was used for the occasion, the floor of the saloon not being safe ever since Robert Adam removed the pillars his father had put in to support it, so that the chandelier below shook even when someone walked across the saloon floor. The Menottis after acquiring the house have finally solved the problem by putting in steel girders at great cost and effort.

There was a piper, accordionist and drummer, if I remember correctly and the evening usually commenced with a 'Dashing White Sergeant' and continued mainly with reels like the 'Eightsome and Foursome reel' the former of which the tenants danced with great gusto swinging through the 'Figure of Eight' which the family sedately danced through. I danced the 'Gay Gordons' with a dark haired man off the estate and was much taken by him. Other dances included the 'Petronella' and 'Hamilton House' which has been one of my favourites ever since, also daces like 'Paul Jones' and the 'Military Two Step' to ensure everyone joined in.

At midnight a piper piped in the New Year and we all drank quite disgusting rum punch made with tea and rum before going safely to bed.

After New year eventually came the sad day to leave for the south and our respective schools. Hugo thought of the ingenious method of he and I writing our 'thank you letters' on the afternoon preceding our departure, on Yester writing paper, and posting our letters as we left through Gifford, thus gaining favour with Aunt Marjorie since our letters then arrived first, in particular before that of cousin Frances who lived in London.

SOLDIERS EPITAPH
*"They died together
That we might live forever"*

CHAPTER III
YESTER AT WAR

I have a drawing executed by Johnny Churchill, Winston's nephew in 1939, depicting Yester House. There is a clump of trees to the right of the house where the drawing room and yellow sitting room are situated. There are four planes in the air above it. Two of the planes look as if they are about to dive bomb the house and the other two flying away from it towards the Lammermuirs. These two were in fact German planes and subsequently one was shot down over Humbie in the Lammermuir Hills. I believe it was the first enemy plane to be shot down on British soil during World War II.

Another story behind this picture is that the pilots and aircrew stationed at Drem during the war used to come to Yester for weekends and when off duty to rest. There were several daughters of the 11th Marquis of Tweeddale and other young ladies resident at the house at that time, all sheltering from the blitz with their children. They naturally became friends of the airmen who as a token of friendship and to tease them, but also for a dare, used to fly between the trees and the house when in that direction of missions and exercises.

One of these missions however ended quite abruptly. One day my grandmother, the Marchioness of Tweeddale, saw a plane in obvious trouble flying above the park in front of the house. Eventually two parachutes were

THE CHILDREN OF YESTER

Yester House by Johnny Churchill

seen descending from this with two airmen. My grandmother, thinking they were Germans, armed herself with a shotgun and advanced on the men. At her approach, gun in hand, two very young men got shakily to their feet raising their arms above their heads in token of surrender. "Please don't shoot", they said, "We're not Germans, we're the pilots from Drem on our first solo flight, the plane began to stutter and we weren't sure why, but thought we might be going to run out of fuel and we couldn't remember which was the fuel guage. Our Commander Beahy has told us 'pilots are more valuable than planes', so we thought we had better get out before it crashed". Luckily the plane reached the Lammermuirs before it did crash and so came down without doing anyone any harm. My grandmother took them back to the house and rang Drem. When their commander duly arrived to fetch them, the pilots nervously stood to attention and repeated what he had said to them. He replied coldly, "Yes, but you're not pilots, are you?" and took them back to base.

CHAPTER IV
ETIQUETTE AND MANNERS OF DAYS GONE BY

After we had both gone to Boarding school for a year or two Nanny left us and went to look after the Russak family in Haddington. The nursery was closed except for the top play room and the war being ended most of the other 16 children and their nannies went back to their own homes and when visiting later were usually housed in the main house.

Once one had graduated into the main house one was free to come and go as one liked, but expected to adhere to the manners and customs of the house. Punctuality and good manners and deference for ones elders was expected but the wants and needs of the young were also respected, as was that of the servants. Aunt Marjorie on the whole organising every thing but Grandpa quietly in control and slipping in with a quiet word when needed. "That's Quite enough" from Grandpa was enough to stop anyone in their tracks.

Breakfast was the least formal meal, other than tea, and was at nine o'clock, for which one was called at eight o'clock by the house maids opening one's curtains and in the case of the adults being given early morning tea. However one was not considered late unless one arrived after Grandpa. Grandpa always had orange juice served in a glass jug on the side and after he had taken his, but not until, we were allowed to drink any left over. There was toast in little silver toast racks on the table and everyone had their own little butter dish with rolled pats of butter in front of each place.

At the side serving table was coffee and a choice of cooked breakfast, for example:-Porridge followed by kippers; kedgeree - a favourite, mixed grill or scrambled eggs, to which one helped oneself; and fresh fruit like peaches and nectarines on the dessert side board to finish up with.

In the war there was a very limited side table because of rationing, and Grandpa Einstein, Granny's Foster Father, came to stay from being abroad where there was no rationing and coming down early to breakfast one day helped himself to everything on the sideboard, thinking the limited amount was one portion whereas it was meant to go round everyone!

Grandpa and Aunt Marjorie sat in armchairs at either end of the vast elongated table with the family and guests ranged along the sides. In the middle of the table was a large silver model depicting the Battle of Luncarty at which the Hay family turned the fleeing Scots and together defeated the Danes who until that moment were carelessly celebrating their victory over them. This had been given to the 8th Marquis of Tweeddale when the Governor of Madras.

The Dogs came to meals and Aunt Marjorie's usually sat behind her or on other people laps. In Granny's day Aunt Helen had a large Great Dane and when between the setting of the table and everyone coming down to breakfast the little butter pats in front of each place began to disappear, he was blamed, until one day the table was improperly dusted and in the dust was a route of tiny dog's footprints from Grannie's chair right along the table stopping at each butter dish until it reached Grandpa's and the true culprit was discovered, Grannie's miniature Pomeranian who had learnt the route on being sent across the table top to get his bit toast each morning from Grandpa!

There was an additional partaker of breakfast toast and that was "Ciggy" the swan who lived for years on the burn at the back of the house. Each morning he would ascend the curved slope up to the dining room windows - the original front entrance to the house and tap on the windows for his daily share of toast. He lived alone for years until a mate was found for him. When a female swan with a broken wing was found on the road and joined him there. But by the time I had grown up they had both disappeared and, sadly, left no descendants.

Aunt Marjorie had a thing about red clothes and so for years the colour was banned at meals, apart from the Hay Tartan, until one morning having given me a red petticoat for Christmas, Grandpa appeared in red as did several others of us by mutual consent - me in red corduroys, for breakfast, and after that no more was said.

After breakfast one was free to go about ones own devices as long as one appeared for lunch, hair brushed, hands washed and in tidy clothes i.e. no jeans for the men and skirts, not trousers, for the ladies. Lunch was heralded by Ned ringing the gong and punctuality was expected but one was not actually considered late until the company had moved from the yellow room into the dining room after which one could expect a reproof or sarcastic comment from Aunt Marjorie.

Once the house was open to the public in the afternoon, at weekends punctuality was even more imperative, but I had great difficulty in arriving on time for lunch since I worked in the City Hospital in Edinburgh until at least 12 o'clock. Ned, however, always protective would greet me at the front door kindly saying;- "It's all right they've not gone through yet", or if I was later "They've gone through, you'd better hurry, leave your car and I'll park it for you."

At lunch which was more formal Ned waited on us bringing the vegetables and pudding to be taken from the left side without making a mess or dropping any food. As I have said the first Lady guest sat on Grandpa's right and the person sitting next to her was said to be in "starvation corner" since they were served last and one got into trouble if one did not leave more than enough for them.

Dinner too was formal and after dessert the ladies would leave the men to their cigars and stories and withdraw to tidy themselves upstairs and wait for the men in the yellow room or on more formal occasions in the drawing room. The men relieved themselves in the downstairs loo which led off the hall, though in the old days one of the sideboards had a side cupboard with a receptacle in it so that the men did not even have to leave the dining room to do so.

Deference to elder was expected at all times. The young and especially the males would open the doors for the ladies who went through first and the young were expected to stand up when an older adult came into the room, especially if a lady, and offer their chairs if necessary. The aunts and great aunts would often stand in front of the fires, and I'm told in Victorian days would "up their bustles" thus warming their behinds. In fact the 8th Marquis of Tweeddale died after falling into the fire in the yellow sitting room but how that happened I don't know.

Great Granny Wagg and Great Aunt Clemmy were the oldest Ladies in the house and would usually sit on the drawing room sofa together and comment on each others frailties if either left the room.

When going out in cars the adults naturally sat in the front and on buses we were taught as children to get up and offer our seats to any adult standing, especially to the old and infirm.

CHAPTER V
EVENTS, TRIALS AND TRIBULATIONS

After the end of the war, when I was about four years old, my father came to Yester for the last time bringing with him presents from Italy where he had been stationed:- the doll china tea set, mentioned before, and a large doll complete with collapsible high chair

He took Nanny, Hugo and me up North Berwick Law which stands to the south-west of the modern housing estate on the outskirts of North Berwick. Having parked our car we walked up the path that ascends the West or landward side of the hill, past stunted gorse bushes which turn the lower slopes of the hill yellow in Spring, and rising slowly then more steeply to the top where there stands the ruins of a once lived in cottage. From here one gets a breath taking view of the white streaked Bass Rock, a mile and a half out to sea, and right across the Firth to the shores of Fife and back across the farming plains of East Lothian to Edinburgh and Arthur's Seat. However I was too cold and miserable to fully appreciate what one could see of this scene, since it started to snow on our way up and I being very susceptible to the cold, cried for most of the way, though my brother being eighteen months older and stronger enjoyed it.

Another event devastated by snow was, I remember, a few years later when I travelled up from London to Scotland without my family since our schools broke up on different dates and mummy and Hugo had already arrived at Yester. Instead I was accompanied on the train by two school friends, Caroline who was my age and Linda Arthur her older sister. However the snow caused a derailment at Newcastle so we had to change trains at Doncaster and go direct to Glasgow instead of Edinburgh. After many hours of delay and waiting in the freezing carriage. It so happened we had the old style two seated carriage to ourselves, but being exceedingly bored we fought over my dolls most of the way and eventually arrived in Glasgow well after midnight, where nanny and Mrs Arthur had come to meet us and since we were so late put up for the night in the Glasgow Railway Hotel before being driven back to Yester later the following day.

Conversely another exceptional event was one of my brother, Hugo's, birthdays when Margaret Sullavan, American actress and Kenneth Wagg's second wife was staying at Yester. She organised Hugo's birthday and practically bought up the whole of Gifford for it. Never had I seen so many presents and sweets let alone Hugo whose birthday it was! They included packets of the American invention Spearmint Chewing Gum, much to Aunt Marjories disgust who forbade it being eaten in the house. In defiance of the adults therefore we used to sit on the stone pedestals at the back entrance to the house openly chewing it and pulling it into long strips in a disgusting manner.

It was at this birthday, I think that Hugo was given a set of Pelham Puppets which included Queen, King, Black Witch and a super Red Devil complete with a stage on which we used to give performances with them to the adults.

CHAPTER VI
SUMMER HOLIDAYS

    In the summer outdoor pursuits were encouraged as much as possible. There were swings and a huge sea saw on the nursery lawn for the smaller children and grass tennis courts in front of the house and a croquet lawn at the back of the house for the older children and adults. The Waggs excelled at Tennis.

    Once we had grown out of Nanny's supervision we invented a game during which we had to climb round the outside of the house whilst maintaining contact with the main wall. This entailed climbing up the sides of the drawing room steps and onto some of the window sills at the back of the house as it was built on two levels. Needless to say the adults were unaware of this somewhat dubious activity.

    Tricycles were gradually replaced by bicycles for which we devised various racing circuits including one in which we pedalled as fast as we could from the house to the bridge, where the road divided into front and back drive, and then freewheeled as far as we could down the rest of the main drive until our bicycles came to a standstill or we fell off. Whoever got the furthest was the winner.

    We also walked for miles in the woods both with Nanny and later, when we were older, led by Hugo when we also walked up the Burns. This latter activity was frowned upon by the adults when I fell in and returned wet. There were magnificent trees in the woods and drive including some of the oldest Beeches and Larches in Scotland and plenty of nuts as well as wild strawberries to be gathered in season. There was also a Monkey Puzzle tree alas long since gone.

One day we - Anthony and David Wagg, Hugo and I - decided to cross the half fallen down bridge across the old lake, near the old riding stables erected by the 8th Marquis, to explore the small island in the middle. Unfortunately, there was a wasps nest hidden between the planks of the bridge and we, especially David, all got stung and fell out with Aunt Marjorie for our foolhardy adventure.

There were also more organised activities planned by Nanny and later Aunt Marjorie. We used to be taken paddling on the lovely sandy beaches of North Berwick complete with bucket and spade and spent hours constructing sand castles with moats for the tide to fill and eventually destroy.

Hugo and Vicky on tricycle

THE CHILDREN OF YESTER

We also went mackerel fishing in the sea in the fisherman's open boats which usually had a few small crabs clambering around inside and I can well remember the excitement of pulling up the lines heavy with caught fish.

Hugo and Vicky at North Berwick

THE CHILDREN OF YESTER

Once I can remember going to a Fete in North Berwick where there was a pipe band and from then on I was determined to be a drum major or at least a majorette and practised for hours marching up and down the lawn twirling sticks.

Grandpa was Lord Lieutenant of East Lothian but we rarely accompanied him when on official duty, the one time Aunt Marjorie did explains the reason why:

Aunt Marjorie took the Wagg children, Hugo and I to a Swimming Gala at North Berwick which has an open air swimming pool. We children sat on benches at the front to watch the races and behaved as if butter would not melt in our mouths until the Lord Provost came to announce the prize giving and declared in a loud pompous voice:- "And now the Marchioness of TWADLE will present the prizes" at which we almost fell off our seats with laughing.

Grandpa took the salute at the Tattoo in Edinburgh for several years but although we went we were usually sent on another night and sat on the stands with the general public not in the Royal Box, though Hugo was once taken by Aunt Helen and Uncle Lionel to sit in the Press box with them. No television viewing of the Tattoo can beat the feeling of going to it live and sitting usually shivering on ones cushion, if one remembered to take one, and watching the marvellous bands and displays against the back drop of the castle.

After August 12th there was of course Grouse shooting on the Lammermuirs in which the older Waggs took part but we did not.

CHAPTER VII
GRANDPA'S DEATH

Grandpa died at Yester, aged 82, after a prolonged illness following a broken leg on 30th March, 1967 and a Memorial Service was held for him on Monday 3rd April in St. Mary's Haddington at 11.30 a.m.

Unfortunately, I had been asked to a debutante ball by my cousin Catherine Berry that weekend and as we were going in a large house party, I had to go, though Aunt Helen and Uncle Lionel went straight to Yester the minute they heard the news. I was feeling very miserable as I had loved Grandpa and also felt that part of my world had come to an end. As we entered the ballroom we were greeted by young Lord Aboyne who said to Catherine 'Sorry to hear of your Grandfather's death'. This was too much for me and I burst into tears and as I was not dancing crept up into a gallery when I could cry in private. There eventually, Desmond Alexander found me and took me down to dance but even he could not cheer me up and as far as I was concerned the dance was a fiasco.

Early on Monday morning I and the rest of the family caught a plane from London to Edinburgh where Anthony Wagg was detailed to drive me to Haddington though some of the family went straight to Yester first which Anthony did not want to do.

The service was held in the west end of St. Mary's as in those days the east end was still a ruin open to the sky. Over 50 friends and relatives attended and the Queen was represented by Admiral Sir Peter Reid Vice Lieutenant of East Lothian. The service was conducted by the Rev. Robert Dollar, Minister of Dunfermline, assisted by the Rev. J.S. Thomson and the Rev. G.D. Monro. The service started with the hymn 'The Lord's my shepherd' and continued with 'To be a pilgrim' and ended with 'Abide with me', the latter of which for years afterwards I could not hear without feeling sad and thinking of Grandpa's funeral.

After the service, we joined the long slow funeral cortege back to Gifford and Yester and I was very touched when a farmer ploughing his land by the road side, stopped his tractor and stood by the gate of the field cap in hand as the funeral cortege drove by. Eventually we got to Yester where Grandpa was interred in St. Cuthberts, the chapel next to the house to which we retired for refreshments.

As Grandpa had no living son and therefore single heir the estate had to be sold to pay death duties including the house. The Estate was bought for over £25,000.00 by Dr. Innes Lumsden who had already bought and was living at Quarryford Farm which had originally been part of the estate.

He sold Yester House to 'the boys' Mr. Derek Parker and Mr. Peter Morris, interior designers and antique dealers who continued to live at the Hopes which they had also bought and in their turn let back Yester House itself to Aunt Marjorie Tweeddale who stayed at Yester till December 1969 when she gave it up and went after a short stay in London to live at Oddington in Gloucestershire in February 1970. From there she moved to Tangier Morocco by 1972 where she died in 1977.

Meantime after a few years of living in it themselves 'the Boys' sold Yester House to Gian Carlo Menotti in 1973 who was an owner and occupier together with his adopted son Francis 'Chips' Menotti and daughter-in-law Melinda. Francis has since sold the house to the Wood family.

CHAPTER VIII
OPEN TO THE PUBLIC

On June the First 1968 Aunt Marjorie opened Yester House to the public. In preparation for this my mother had gone through 35 drawers of letters, charters and papers in Grandpa's business room and from there wrote a guide book about the house and family portraits on show, plus additional more detailed notes for the guides in each room. The papers were then given to the Records Office and National Library in Edinburgh. Aunt Marjorie also compiled a book of recipes, used over the years at Yester, to be sold in the shop.

The rooms shown to the public were: The dining room and the double drawing room; then up the main staircase into the saloon and upstairs sitting room. The downstairs bedroom called 'the boudoir' was turned into a shop selling antiques, tweeds, handknits, gifts and produce from the garden and teas with homebaked cakes and scones were served in one of the basement rooms.

The house was opened from June the first until October the 15th from 2-5.30 p.m. on Thursdays, Fridays, Saturdays and Sundays and bus parties were catered for by arrangement, usually in the week. The entrance fee to the house was 3/6d and the same amount again was paid for tea.

THE CHILDREN OF YESTER

The weekend guides consisted of my mother and stepfather who took the entrance money; myself, two Edinburgh friends of mine Patty and Roddy Martine; Grandpa's niece Lady Marioth Hay and Miss Elizabeth Young who usually managed the shop.

She had originally came to Yester to help look after Grandpa and had stayed on after his death as companion/house keeper. Staff from the estate helped with the teas and Aunt Marjorie supervised overall whilst we guided each around one room.

We found all who came very appreciative and contrary to warnings nothing was ever taken except once Aunt Marjorie's handbag was taken from the 'yellow' sitting room when a booked private party was going

Mummy (Lady Daphne Stewart) and I at Stewart Society dinner

round and was later found emptied of contents in the woods.

On Saturday July 20th a Fete was held in the grounds of Yester in front of the house in aid of the Lamp of Lothian Collegiate Centre, and was opened by Sir Learie Constantine M.B.E., High Commissioner of Trinidad and Tobago and Rector of St. Andrews University.

On the 4th November 1968 the Stewart Society to which my stepfather, mother and myself belonged, held its triennial dinner at Yester to which we all went, the company numbering 45 in all. We were piped into dinner in the dining room by Pipe Major Davidson (Scots Guards) and after dinner Aunt Marjorie proposed the toast to the Stewart Society and in return Lord Galloway, the Hon. President proposed the toast of Lady Tweeddale and the Hays of Yester. My mother then replied for the Hays explaining that the Hays of Yester were related to the Royal Stewarts by descent from the daughter of King Robert II and recited a poem she had made up for the occasion and gave a brief history of the Hays of Yester up to the time of the 45. She then guided the party around the house before we ended the evening by dancing an Eightsome and a Foursome reel in the hall.

This must have been one of the last formal dos held at Yester before Aunt Marjorie left for England in December, 1969.

THE CHILDREN OF YESTER